To our dearest Hani, great journey Mubarak for [...] acceptance and eternal [...]

Advice for the Student

of

Knowledge

Some useful advice for those who are studying
sacred Islamic knowledge.

By
Shaykh Mufti Saiful Islām

JKN Publications

First Edition October 2012 - 3000 copies
Second Edition September 2016 - 3000 copies

ISBN 978-1-909114-00-5

British Library Cataloguing in Publication Data
A catalogue record for this book is available from the British Library.

Publisher's Note:

Every care and attention has been put into the production of this book. If however, you find any errors, they are our own, for which we seek Allāh's ﷻ forgiveness and reader's pardon.

Published by:

JKN Publications
118 Manningham Lane
Bradford
West Yorkshire
BD8 7JF
United Kingdom

t: +44 (0) 1274 308 456 | w: www.jkn.org.uk | e: info@jkn.org.uk

Book Title: Advice for the Students of Knowledge

Author: Shaykh Mufti Saiful Islām

Printed by Mega Printing in Turkey

"In the Name of Allāh, the Most Beneficent,
the Most Merciful"

Contents

Preface

All praise be to Allāh ﷻ the Lord of the Worlds, and may infinite peace and blessings be showered upon His last and Final Messenger, Muhammad ﷺ, his noble family, his noble Companions ﷺ and upon those who follow their path until the Day of Judgement.

Etiquettes and mannerism plays an integral role in our Deen. It constitutes almost twenty percent of our religion, so we can imagine how vast this topic is. It has always been the tradition of our pious predecessors to primarily inculcate into the student of Deen mannerism and the fundamental etiquettes of seeking knowledge. Hence, in order for a student of Deen to excel and attain blessings in knowledge, he is required to inculcate into himself the etiquettes of seeking sacred Islamic knowledge. This is because to attain this knowledge one is not required to have a good memory or a sharp mind, but relatively to observe the etiquettes of seeking knowledge as Allāh ﷻ gives in abundance on the account of mannerism.

This tradition has continued right from the noble era of the Messenger ﷺ. The noble Sahābah ﷺ would sit with utmost respect and observe great mannerism and etiquettes when the Holy Prophet ﷺ would deliver a sermon. Sayyidunā Suhail Ibn Amr ﷺ (who was not yet a Muslim) relates his observation of the Sahābah's ﷺ utmost respect towards the Messenger of Allāh ﷺ on the occasion of the treaty of Hudaibiyah.

6

He himself relates that whenever the Holy Prophet ﷺ would deliver a speech, they would sit still and listen attentively with such respect as if a bird was perched on their heads.

Moreover, there are many accounts related about the great scholars of the past of how cautious they were in observing good mannerism when seeking knowledge. It was on the account of Ādāb that Allāh ﷻ took great services from them and whose works exist even today to benefit the Ummah.

I express my gratitude to Shaykh Mufti Saiful Islām (may Allāh ﷻ preserve him and prolong his life) for addressing this important matter and explaining the etiquettes of seeking knowledge particularly for those who are seeking knowledge in the traditional Islamic institutes. May Allāh ﷻ grant us the true understanding and the ability to act upon what has been mentioned in this booklet. Āmeen

Mufti Abdul Waheed
Teacher of Fiqh at Jāmiah Khātamun Nabiyyeen
August 2012, Ramadhān 1433

Virtues of Knowledge

"Allāh will raise up to (suitable) ranks (and degrees), those of you who believe and have been granted knowledge. And Allāh is well-acquainted with all you do." (58:11)

Sayyidunā Uthmān Ibn Affān ؓ narrated that the Holy Prophet ﷺ said, "The most superior among you are those who learn the Holy Qur'ān and teach it." (Bukhāri)

Sayyidunā Abdur-Rahmān Ibn Abū Bakra's ؓ father narrated that the Holy Prophet ﷺ said, "If Allāh ﷻ wants to do good to a person, He makes him comprehend the religion and of course knowledge is attained by learning." (Bukhāri)

Sayyidunā Abū Hurairah ؓ narrates that the Holy Prophet ﷺ said, "He who treads the path in search of knowledge, Allāh ﷻ will make that path easy leading to Paradise for him. And those who assemble in one of the houses of Allāh ﷻ (Masājid), recite the Book of Allāh ﷻ and learn and teach the Holy Qur'ān (among themselves), there will descend upon them tranquillity and mercy will cover them. The angels will surround them and Allāh ﷻ will mention them in the presence of those near Him. He who is slow-paced in doing good deeds, his (noble) descent does not make him go ahead." (Muslim)

Sayyidunā Hasan Basri ؓ narrates that the Holy Prophet ﷺ said, "The superiority of a scholar, who observes the prescribed prayer

8

and then sits down to teach people goodness, over the worshipper who observes fast during the day and worships during the night, is like my superiority over the lowest in rank amongst you." (Tirmizi)

Sayyidunā Abdullāh Ibn Abbās ؓ narrated that the Holy Prophet ﷺ said, "A single scholar of religion is more formidable against Shaytān than a thousand devout people." (Tirmizi, Ibn Mājah)

Sayyidunā Abdullāh Ibn Abbās ؓ narrated that the Holy Prophet ﷺ said, "Acquiring knowledge in company for an hour in the night is better than spending the whole night in prayer." (Tirmizi)

He showed to us the noble status of the learned people of his Ummah. Sayyidunā Abū Umāmah ؓ relates that the Holy Prophet ﷺ said, "A learned one is as much above an (ordinary) worshipper as I am above the least of you," and he added, "Allāh ﷻ, His angels and all those in the heavens and in the earth, even the ants in their holes and the fish in the water, call down blessings on those who instruct people in beneficent knowledge." (Tirmizi)

Sayyidunā Abdullāh Ibn Abbās ؓ said, "The scholars have stations which are seven hundred ranks above the (ordinary) believers, and between each rank is a distance of a five hundred year journey."

Allāh ﷻ states in the Holy Qur'ān, **"Only the knowledgeable from among Allāh's slaves fear Him."** (35: 28)

It is reported in Bukhāri and Muslim, through the Hadeeth of Say-yidunā Mu'āwiyah ﷺ who said, "I heard the Holy Prophet ﷺ say, 'Whomsoever Allāh ﷻ wishes well for, He gives him understand-ing in religion'." (Bukhāri)

In another Hadeeth it is reported, "The superiority of the scholar over the worshipper is like the superiority of the night of the full moon over the rest of the heavenly bodies. And the scholars are the heirs of the Prophets. The Prophets do not endow gold coins nor silver coins. They only endow knowledge, so whoever takes hold of it has taken an ample share." (Abū Dāwood)

Sayyidunā Abū Hurairah ﷺ narrates that the Holy Prophet ﷺ said, "Whoever travels upon a path seeking knowledge thereupon, Allāh ﷻ will ease for him thereby a path to Heaven." (Muslim)

Furthermore, it is stated in another Hadeeth, "Whoever meets with death while seeking knowledge with which to revive Islām, there will be only a single rank separating him from the Prophets in Heaven." (Dārimi)

"Allāh will exalt those who have faith among you and those who have knowledge to high ranks." (58:11)

Those learned men who are strong in the pursuit of knowledge and understanding are those who guide others. They have a great responsibility and thus their rank is high. The Prophets ﷺ were men of wisdom and Divine Knowledge, and it was this gift from

10

Allāh ﷻ which gave them the ability to guide others to the straight path. Gaining knowledge is such an essential part of Islām that even in Jihād (Holy War), where fighting maybe inevitable, Allāh ﷻ 'orders' a party to remain behind for the purpose of study, so that when the fighters return home, the sanctity of Islamic knowledge will remain safe.

"And the Believers should not all go out to fight; of every troop of them, a party only should go forth, that they (who are left behind) may gain sound knowledge in religion, and that they may warn their folk when they return to them, so that they may beware." (9:122)

"O my Lord! Increase me in knowledge." (20:114)

After reading all these promises and glad tidings, one might ask, what more do we need to awaken our consciousness? We have been promised an easy way to Paradise; the inheritance of our Holy Prophet ﷺ; a lofty rank, high and noble in status; a blessing from Allāh ﷻ and a supplication of all that exists in the heavens and earth; a face beaming in brightness and beauty on the Day of Judgement when other faces will be sad and dismal.

So let us embark on the road to Paradise; let us seek knowledge today.

Ten Etiquettes of Seeking Islamic Knowledge

My beloved students! It is the beginning of the academic year, hence I have gathered you all to mention some of the etiquettes of seeking knowledge. Great scholars have discussed many etiquettes of learning. I will mention the ten most essential etiquettes for seeking sacred Islamic knowledge:

1. Correct Intention

Whatever a person does in his or her life, the single most important thing is to do that thing (the action or deed) with a correct and sincere intention. This is especially important for a student of Islamic knowledge since the value of all the time spent as a student will be measured and accounted for according to whether it was done for the pleasure of Allāh ﷻ or whether it was done for any other motive.

The importance of having a correct intention is highlighted in the following two Ahādeeth of the Holy Prophet ﷺ:

Hadeeth 1:

اِنَّمَا الْاَعْمَالُ بِالنِّيَّاتِ وَاِنَّمَا لِكُلِّ امْرِئٍ مَّا نَوٰى فَمَنْ كَانَتْ هِجْرَتُهُ اِلَى اللّٰهِ وَرَسُوْلِهٖ فَهِجْرَتُهُ
اِلَى اللّٰهِ وَرَسُوْلِهٖ وَمَنْ كَانَتْ هِجْرَتُهُ اِلَى الدُّنْيَا يُصِيْبُهَا اَوْ اِلَى امْرَأَةٍ يَنْكِحُهَا فَهِجْرَتُهُ
اِلٰى مَا هَاجَرَ اِلَيْهِ (متفق عليه)

"The deeds are considered by the intentions, and a person will get the reward according to his intention. So whoever migrated for Allāh ﷻ and His Messenger ﷺ, his migration will be for Allāh ﷻ and His Messenger ﷺ; and whoever migrated for worldly benefits or for a woman to marry, his migration will be what he migrated for." (Bukhāri, Muslim)

Hadeeth 2:

مَنْ تَعَلَّمَ عِلْمًا مِمَّا يُبْتَنَى بِهِ وَجْهُ اللهِ لَا يَتَعَلَّمُهُ إِلَّا لِيُصِيبَ بِهِ عَرَضًا

مِّنَ الدُّنْيَا لَمْ يَجِدْ عَرْفَ الْجَنَّةِ يَوْمَ الْقِيَامَةِ يَعْنِى رِيْحَهَا

(ابو داود و ابن ماجة)

"Whosoever learns that knowledge by which Allāh's ﷻ pleasure is sought, only to acquire by it worldly goods will not smell the scent of Paradise on the Day of Judgement i.e. its fragrance."

(Abū Dāwood, Ibn Mājah)

Remember the story regarding the great scholar, Imām Ghazāli ﷫ when he enrolled into a Madrasah to learn knowledge. The king who was the guardian of the Madrasah, one day visited the Madrasah disguised as a normal person in order to see the progress of the Madrasah. When the king asked the students why they were there, he got answers like, "My father is a famous doctor and I also want to become a doctor," "My parents forced me to come here," "I only came here for the free food and accommodation."

Disheartened with the answers the king started to believe that the Madrasah was a waste of time and effort and began considering closing it down. As he was leaving, he came across a student sitting alone and studying with humility and great concentration, so he asked him what he was doing there.

"O boy! why have you decided to study?" The young boy surprised by the question replied, "What a strange question! I am too busy to respond to your question, however I will answer you. I study for the pleasure of Allāh ﷻ. On hearing this answer, the king decided to keep the Madrasah open just for the sake of that one student who he was not to know would become known as "Hujjatul Islām"(the proof of Islam) the great Imām Ghazāli ﷺ.

So our intention for studying should always be correct and we should make it a habit to regularly verify our intention. It should not be for a worldly title or status but only for the pleasure of Allāh ﷻ, otherwise our time spent will be futile. Imām Ghazāli ﷺ also spent 10 years away from society in the pursuit of spiritual rectification and enlightenment.

2. Etiquettes in Relation to the Teacher

There are a number of essential etiquettes which a student needs to adhere to in order to gain the maximum benefit from the studies.

Itā'at (Obedience) - This is the student doing as advised by the teacher without question, whether in agreement or not.

14

Khidmat - Helping or serving the teacher.

Azmat - Honouring the teacher outwardly and inwardly and never talking negatively in relation to the teacher.

Practical examples:

- Not to point one's feet in the direction of the teacher.
- Not to sit in the company of the teacher without a head garment (hat, turban etc.).
- Not to sit with one's back facing the teacher.
- Not to engage in arguments, debates or disagreements with the teacher.
- Maintaining good punctuality.
- Having the presence of the mind and soul during lessons ensuring that full concentration is given.

Not showing disapproval at being rebuked by the teacher

Any sign of annoyance at being told off by the teacher could be construed as a sign of pride as this feeling of annoyance often stems from pride. Pride is a very difficult thing to comprehend but it is sufficient for a student to remember that a person in whose heart is pride can never acquire true knowledge. It is the very reason that Shaytān disobeyed Allāh ﷻ when he was asked to bow down to Prophet Ādam ﷺ. Even though Shaytān had vast and concrete knowledge of Allāh ﷻ and His creation, it was of no use to him because the pride in his heart led to his disobedience and ultimately him being accursed and outcaste. A Hadeeth of the Holy Prophet ﷺ mentions that a person having even an atom's weight of pride in his heart shall not enter Paradise.

Etiquettes are a quality which have been emphasised by the Holy Prophet ﷺ verbally and through action.

Example 1:

Once on a journey with some Companions ؓ the Holy Prophet ﷺ enquired regarding a tall structure that they came across which was being built. The Companions ؓ informed him (the Holy Prophet ﷺ) whose structure it was. Later when that Companion ؓ (the owner of the structure) met the Holy Prophet ﷺ and greeted him, the Holy Prophet ﷺ turned away from him. Realising that there must be a reason for the Holy Prophet's ﷺ displeasure, that Companion ؓ asked the others what the reason was. They informed him of the journey and the tall structure. He then immediately went and demolished the structure without questioning and without feeling the need to inform the Holy Prophet ﷺ that he had demolished it.

Example 2:

On one occasion the Holy Prophet ﷺ saw a Companion ؓ wearing a gold ring. The Holy Prophet ﷺ physically removed the ring from the Companion's ؓ finger and threw it away. Later after the Holy Prophet ﷺ had gone, the other Companions ؓ advised him to pick up the ring and sell it or use it for something else. But that Companion ؓ said, "I will never pick up something that the Holy Prophet ﷺ has thrown away with his blessed hands."

16

3. Etiquettes of the Books

There are a number of etiquettes pertaining to the books which a student should always keep in mind.

- Not to rest on the books.
- Not to turn one's back towards the books.
- Consider the stacking order of the books:
- (From top) Tafseer → Hadeeth → Fiqh → Nahw →
  → Sarf → Mantiq etc. (to bottom) - This is the order mentioned by Shaykh Ashraf Ali Thānwi ﷺ.
- The student should ensure that he/she is always in the state of Wudhu.

It is also related regarding Shaykh Anwar Shāh Kashmīri ﷺ that he respected his books to the extent that after placing a book on the table to study he would not rotate the book for his own ease but instead he would leave the book in its place and move around the table himself in order to read some commentary or footnotes. Due to this respect in relation to his books, Allāh ﷻ blessed him with such knowledge that he carried the title of 'The Walking Library'.

4. Etiquettes of the Madrasah

There are a number of etiquettes pertaining to the Madrasah which a student should keep in mind.

- Never to complain about the facilities.

- Never to complain about the teachers.
- Never to complain about the food or provisions.
- To keep it clean and tidy at all times and be grateful.
- Always to have respect for all other institutions of knowledge and not only the one being attended.
- Always be willing to help in the maintenance and the well being of the Madrasah.
- Always be willing to participate in the Madrasah activities such as fundraising etc.
- Always be humble and grateful for the opportunity given by Allāh ﷻ to study Deen whatever the circumstances.

Shaykh Abdul Qādir Raipūri ﷺ had nothing during his student days not even a blanket. He used whatever old tattered cloth he could find for a blanket and this practice of simplicity and humility continued throughout his entire days as a student.

5. Respect for the Teacher

Consider every teacher as a mercy from Allāh ﷻ. It is perfectly acceptable to favour one teacher over another but the utmost respect for all the teachers is paramount as they are all a means for the student to attain the knowledge which is a light from Allāh ﷻ.

6. Respect for all the Scholars of Fiqh (Jurisprudence)

Not to lose respect for any Faqeeh (scholar of Jurisprudence) during learning and discussing their various differences of opinion in relation to certain issues. Especially when proving one opinion to be superior over another. Consequently not to utter any words which may be perceived as belittling such as: "That is easy! How could he not have understood that?" or "I cannot believe that he said that!"

7. Salutations upon the Holy Prophet ﷺ

Send Durood (salutations) upon the Holy Prophet ﷺ in abundance. Also it is important to say *'Radhiyallāhu anhu'* when the name of any Sahābi is mentioned and *'Rahmatullāhi alayhi'* for the scholars.

8. To Seek Help from Allāh ﷻ

Seek help from Allāh ﷻ at all times and supplicate regularly for His guidance and His acceptance.

9. To Remain in the State of Wudhu

Always be in a state of ritual purity (Wudhu). Ensure that one's body and clothes are clean. This is of great benefit spiritually, physically and it shows consideration and respect for the fellow students.

10. To Lose the Robe of Pride

It is narrated from Imām Bukhāri ﷺ, "A shy person and a proud person are both deprived of knowledge"

19

There is a well known Arabic phrase:

اَلْعِلْمُ عِزٌّ لَا ذُلَّ فِيْهِ وَيَحْصُلُ بِذُلٍّ لَا عِزَّ فِيْهِ

"Knowledge is respect, there is no disgrace in it at all, and it is acquired through (enduring) disgrace with no respect in it."

Unparalleled Examples of the Pious Predecessors

We should never forget the unparalleled examples of the struggle of the pious predecessors to acquire knowledge. It should be appreciated that nowadays this knowledge in comparison to earlier times, is as if it has been handed to us 'on a plate'. For example we have access to preserved good quality books, the teachers are available to explain them and the buildings and facilities are available to us. The effort made by the Sahābah ﷺ, the Tā'bieen ﷺ, the Mufassiroon ﷺ, the Muhaddithoon ﷺ and many others should not be forgotten.

Keeping in mind their struggle for the acquisition and the preservation of the Deen can act as an encouragement and a motivating force for a person. Some examples are as follows:

20

Sayyidunā Abū Hurairah's ﷺ Knowledge of Ahādeeth

From him there are 5374 Ahādeeth narrations. He gave up every-thing including his family, his home and he dedicated his entire life in the pursuit of Ahādeeth. He regularly used to collapse out of hunger in the vicinity of Masjid Nabawi in Madeenah due to in-tense hunger. People used to think that he suffered from epileptic fits but this misconception is clarified in a Hadeeth of Saheeh Bu-khāri:

$$وَمَا بِیْ اِلاَّ الْجُوْعُ$$

"And there was nothing wrong with me besides hunger."

He would be helpless due to hunger and would ask the other Sahābah ﷺ to take him home and feed him. Due to these great efforts from amongst all the Sahābah ﷺ, Allāh ﷻ made him:

$$اَمِیْرُ الْمُؤْمِنِیْن فِی الْحَدِیْث$$

(Leader of the Believers in Hadeeth)

Sayyidunā Abdullāh Ibn Abbās's ﷺ Pursuit for Knowledge

At a young age he was given the title:

$$حِبْرُ الْاُمَّةِ وَ رَئِیْسُ الْمُفَسِّرِیْن$$

(The Scholar of the Ummah and the Leader of the Mufassiroon)

21

At the time of the passing away of the Holy Prophet ﷺ Sayyidunā Abdullāh Ibn Abbās ؓ was only thirteen years of age. He asked another Sahābi ؓ to accompany him in travelling to seek knowledge from the other senior Sahābah ؓ but he declined believing that the senior Sahābah ؓ would refuse to entertain such young children and there was no need to seek knowledge in the presence of the senior Sahābah ؓ.

Sayyidunā Abdullāh Ibn Abbās ؓ therefore set out in pursuit of his mission alone. He used to visit the senior Sahābah ؓ in the intense heat of the day and if he did not find them he would patiently wait outside their houses covered in sweat and sand but not daring to knock on the door fearing that he may disturb them.

When the Sahābi ؓ would emerge from his house he would see Sayyidunā Abdullāh Ibn Abbās ؓ and say, "O cousin of the Holy Prophet ﷺ why did you not knock on the door? I would have come out of the house for you." Sayyidunā Abdullāh Ibn Abbās ؓ would reply, "No this need is mine."

He remained steadfast upon that principle and practice all his life, only then did he become known as the 'Imām-ul Mufassireen'.

Sayyidunā Jābir's ؓ Journey to Damascus to Acquire Knowledge

It is recorded in Saheeh Bukhāri (in the book of knowledge) that only for the acquisition of one Hadeeth, which he had already heard but wanted to hear it from a Sahābi ؓ who was connected to a 'higher chain', Sayyidunā Jābir ﷺ travelled from Madeenah to Damascus which is approximately a distance of 1500 km. In those days the only means of travel available to people was limited to camel and by foot.

More Examples of Great Sacrifices

In every era, the pious predecessors have made great efforts in the pursuit of knowledge. Saeed Ibn Jubair ﷺ had no money for food, so he bought a kilogram of beans, roasted them and lived on them for one month. He would eat few beans in the morning, afternoon and evening. The rest of his day would be dedicated to learning Ahādeeth. Furthermore, Imām Bukhāri ﷺ never ate any curry for forty years. He would suffice on dry chapatti or four to five almonds. This is mentioned in a book written by Shaykh Abdul Fattāh Abū Guddā ﷺ called:

صَفَحَاتٌ مِنْ صَبْرِ الْعُلَمَاءِ عَلَى شَدَائِدِ الْعِلْمِ وَالتَّحْصِيلِ

"The patience of the scholars facing intense difficulties in the pursuit and the acquisition of knowledge."

He is also the author of other books such as 'The Value of Time' and 'The Great Ulama of the Muslim Ummah' in which he mentions great scholars like Shaykul Islām Ibn Taymiyah ﷺ, Imām Nawawi ﷺ, Imām Tabari ﷺ and others who preferred not to get married but instead dedicated their lives to the acquisition of knowledge.

Such sacrifices can only be made by people who have truly realised and understood the reality of this life and the Hereafter. Due to the sacrifices of our pious predecessors we now have the knowledge preserved and being served to us 'on a plate ready to consume'. All we are required to do is pick up the morsels, chew and swallow them. Unfortunately we are not able to even do that. If we are force fed then we are not able to swallow it, what can be a greater loss than this? This is something worth contemplating upon. We should be grateful and appreciate the ease and the opportunity that has been given to us.

Allāh ﷻ says:

لَاِنْ شَكَرْتُمْ لَاَزِيْدَنَّكُمْ

"If you are grateful, surely I will increase for you." (14:7)

We are able to live normal lives, look after our families, work and still attend Madrasah classes to learn knowledge, often on a flexible basis and at a time that suits us. We should therefore be grateful for this opportunity.

Shaykh Rasheed Ahmad Gangohi ﷺ alone taught the entire Sihah Sitta (six authentic books of Ahādeeth) to his students as there were no other teachers available to facilitate at the time and the students were required to make their own preparations for their livelihoods (food, clothing, shelter etc). Even today there are some places in the Asian sub-continent where the teacher will arrive at a designated destination, teach and then leave. The students are still required to make their own preparations in relation to food, clothing, expenditure and shelter.

Islamic Knowledge Compared to other Knowledge

Islamic knowledge is not like any other knowledge. All other forms of knowledge can be taken directly from books, lectures, audio visual materials and the internet etc. The students can pass and graduate by simply revising prior to the exams. Islamic knowledge (Ilm) is a light (Noor) from Allāh ﷻ. It is pure and is passed on through pure mediums only such as the Angel Jibreel عليه السلام passing it on to the Holy Prophet ﷺ and from the Holy Prophet's ﷺ noble chest to his Companions, the Sahābah ؓ and so on from teacher to student. It has continued in this manner and will continue like this until the end of time.

Books and sermons may facilitate the transfer of knowledge but in essence 'Ilm' is 'Noor' from Allāh ﷻ and He gives it only to whomsoever He wishes.

There is a famous poem regarding Imām Shāfi'ee ؓ when he complained to his teacher Wakee ؒ regarding his weak memory:

شَكَوْتُ اِلٰى وَكِيْعٍ سُوْءَ حِفْظِيْ فَأَوْصَانِيْ اِلٰى تَرْكِ الْمَعَاصِيْ فَاِنَّ الْعِلْمَ نُوْرٌ مِّنْ اِلٰهِيْ

وَ نُوْرُ اللّٰهِ لَا يُعْطٰى لِعَاصِيْ

"I complained to Wakee (my teacher) about my bad memory, he advised me to stop sinning, because indeed knowledge is a light from Allāh 🖼 and the light of Allāh 🖼 is not given to a sinner."

It is also mentioned in a Hadeeth:

$$مَنْ يُّرِدِ اللّٰهُ بِه خَيْراً يُّفَقِّهْهُ فِى الدِّيْنِ$$

"Whoever Allāh 🖼 intends goodness for, He gives him the understanding of Deen (Islām)."

This state is only attained through much repentance and turning towards Allāh 🖼. Hence to attain true knowledge from Allāh 🖼 changes in a student's life are essential. Some important changes are:

- Refraining from sins.
- Increase in worship.
- Abundance of remembrance of Allāh 🖼.
- Abundance of supplication.
- Valuing time.

How to make Du'ā (Supplication to Allāh ﷻ)

Making Du'ā to Allāh ﷻ is a fundamental pillar for achieving success for every Muslim even more so for a student of knowledge. Hence it is vitally important to make Du'ā bearing in mind some essential points. Firstly, acknowledge and admit to Allāh ﷻ that we do not have the ability to acquire the knowledge because of our impure states, our impure tongues and that we are not worthy to utter the blessed name of the Holy Prophet ﷺ let alone reading and conveying his blessed Ahādeeth.

Hence, we must firstly make Du'ā to Allāh ﷻ to give us the means to acquire the knowledge and the sense of appreciation for this great blessing. Also confess that we are not worthy nor deserving of it but we are in need and dependent upon it.

Du'ā should be made in a state of purity with complete humility and devotion knowing fully that the Du'ā is being heard by Allāh ﷻ and that He is the only One that can answer it. Make Du'ā regularly and especially at the 'times of acceptance' like after Salāh, after the recitation of the Holy Qur'ān, after the Asr Salāh on a Friday etc.

27

The Honour and Status of Imām Bukhāri 🙵

Prior to putting pen to paper in relation to any Hadeeth, Imām Bu-khāri 🙵 would perform Ghusl, pray two Rak'ats of Nafl Salāh, make Du'ā Istikhārah and then he would put pen to paper only if his heart inclined towards it.

Even though rightfully we should adhere to this practice, it has be-come impractical to do so. We should at least perform Salāh at night (Salātul-Hājat) invoking Allāh 🙵 to give us the ability to learn His noble Deen. Secondly, we should make a firm intention to learn and act upon every Hadeeth that we read to the best of our ability. Value our time by engaging in the remembrance of Allāh 🙵 (Dhikr) abundantly and by sending salutations upon the Holy Prophet 🙵. We should see it as compulsory that whenever we hear the Holy Prophet's 🙵 name in class or elsewhere that we should send salutations upon him. Thereby inculcating the habit of send-ing salutations into our daily lives on a regular basis.

After making a firm intention and beginning to practise upon it, it is within the human nature to lapse and become forgetful regard-ing one's intention. This should not mean that one should consider this a failure and give up all together but as soon as one remem-bers or is reminded, he should start again as Allāh 🙵 says in the Holy Qur'ān regarding the pious:

تَذَكَّرُوْا فَاِذَا هُمْ مُبْصِرُوْنَ

"When they remember they immediately become aware." (7:201)

وَاِمَّا يَنْزَغَنَّكَ مِنَ الشَّيْطَانِ نَزْغٌ فَاسْتَعِذْ بِاللّٰهِ اِنَّهُ هُوَ السَّمِيْعُ الْعَلِيْمُ

"And if a whisper is whispered to you from the devil, then seek refuge with Allāh. Indeed He is the All-Hearing and the All-Knowing." (7:200)

In the above verse, Allāh ﷺ advises us that if Shaytān the accursed whispers something in order to tempt, distract, confuse or create doubt in the heart or mind of a believer then one should recite:

اَعُوْذُ بِاللّٰهِ مِنَ الشَّيْطَانِ الرَّجِيْمِ

"I seek refuge with Allāh ﷺ from Shaytān the rejected."

Then immediately renew one's intention and continue with a renewed conviction.

It is vital to keep the tongue occupied with the remembrance of Allāh ﷺ and of sending salutations upon the Holy Prophet ﷺ at all times. It is mentioned regarding Hāfiz Ibn Hajar Al-Asqalāni ﷺ, the author of one of the most famous commentaries of Saheeh Bukhāri, 'Fathul-Bāri' that whenever his wooden ink pen became blunt and required sharpening he would perform the Dhikr of Allāh ﷺ while sharpening the pen. He would not waste even a little time by remaining silent.

The Importance of Attending Lessons and its Benefits

A student can be deceived into believing that if he was to miss a lesson then he can catch up by attending other lessons or get the notes from a fellow student or read one of the many books available on the topic. This thought is in fact a big deceit from Shaytān because the method of attaining the knowledge from other than a teacher cannot be compared with the blessings which are attained by taking the knowledge directly from the teacher.

This is because our main objective should be that we hear the Hadeeth via an unbroken chain going all the way to the Holy Prophet ﷺ and thereby become a link in that chain. This method then carries the Light (Noor) of the knowledge (Ilm) which is transferred from heart to heart.

The Golden Chain

When reading Hadeeth there is a statement quoted by the reader which is:

$$وَ بِالسَّنَدِ الْمُتَّصِلِ مِنَّا اِلَى الْاِمَامِ الْبُخَارِيّ ﷺ$$

"By an unbroken chain from us to Imām Bukhāri ﷺ."

This means, that the chain of narrators has been joined to us which goes all the way to the Holy Prophet ﷺ. This chain consists of our teacher, from his teacher, from his teacher and so on all the way to Imām Bukhāri ﵀ who has recorded and preserved the Ahādeeth in a book form. The chain in the book then goes all the way to the Holy Prophet ﷺ which is termed as the 'Golden Chain'. This Golden Chain cannot be acquired by any other means of learning other than the direct student teacher relationship.

It is a blessing from Allāh ﷻ that He enlightens the heart of the student with knowledge taken directly from the revered teacher. The teacher is just a medium used by Allāh ﷻ, Who in reality is the True Bestower of all knowledge. Allāh ﷻ can use any means He sees fit for bestowing knowledge to His servants for example the use of the burning bush for the Prophet Moosā ﵊ and the Angel Jibreel ﵊ for the Holy Prophet ﷺ.

Since there are no more Prophets ﵊ to come now and revelation has been ceased forever, Allāh ﷻ illuminates the hearts of the teachers in response to the interest shown by the students. The blessings in the pursuit of true knowledge and in the desire to recognise one's Lord, results in Allāh ﷻ inspiring the teacher with knowledge which cannot be found in books. As a result, the teacher can sometimes be surprised and amazed as to where the knowledge has emerged from.

This in itself is evidence that real Islamic knowledge (Ilm and Noor) comes from Allāh ﷻ and that it is given to whoever desires it with sincerity resulting in both the teacher and the student benefitting. Due to this sincerity and a real desire to learn, inspiration

31

from Allāh ﷻ is bestowed to a teacher and then it is relayed onto the student.

If this was not the case, then there would be no need for institutions of learning. People could simply study from books, audios, the internet etc. which would result in great confusion and misguidance in the community at large as is very evident in current times.

Punctuality and Attendance

The importance of punctuality and being present throughout the lesson can be realised by looking at the example of Shaykh Muhammad Zakariyya ﷫ during his student days. He had made a firm commitment never to miss any part of the Hadeeth lesson nor be without Wudhu during the lesson. He made a pact with his colleague Shaykh Hasan Ahmad ﷫ that if either one's Wudhu broke, then the other would ask the teacher a question so that whilst the teacher is answering the question, the student would have time to quickly go and renew the Wudhu and return to the class without missing any of the Hadeeth lesson.

This went on for a while without the teacher realising the plan until on one occasion when his colleague Shaykh Hasan Ahmad ﷫ needed to renew his Wudhu, Shaykh Muhammad Zakariyya ﷫ asked a very in-depth and irrelevant question, "Can you explain what Ibnul Humām meant by such and such a statement in his book 'Fathul Qadeer'?"

The teacher understood the reason for the question and paused the teaching of Hadeeth until his colleague returned from performing Wudhu. This commitment continued for the full academic year leading to Shaykh Muhammad Zakariyya ﷺ becoming known as 'Shaykhul Hadeeth'. He wrote many books including the commentary of Muwatta Imām Mālik 'Awjazul Masālik' which is over fifteen volumes long, of the Māliki school of thought and all in Arabic. When it was released and distributed, the Arab scholars after reading it thought that the author must be a great Arab scholar of the Māliki Fiqh and they were intrigued to meet him. They were amazed to discover that he was a Hanafi scholar from the Asian sub continent. Even to this day the book is used in Saudi Arabian universities as a great reference book for the Māliki subjects.

This example of genuine interest for learning along with the required effort shows what can be achieved. It is important to attend regularly and punctually out of the love for the subject rather than just to get an 'attendance tick' in the register.

Deception of Shaytān in the Final Year

Many students in the final year think that because it is the final year and that graduation is usually an automatic procedure at the end of the year, it is not necessary to put as much effort into studying. Nevertheless, the whole of the final year should be dedicated to studying the relevant commentaries and supporting books alongside the lessons. Understanding all the Islamic terminologies, the purpose of each subject, the reasons behind revelations, the background and context of the revelation and the sayings and actions of the Holy Prophet ﷺ, and so on, are very important things to master in the final year.

Fiqh Discussions and Debates

There are many of these in the final year. They all assist in broadening the student's minds and opening up new faculties, however these are not the main objectives. The real objective is 'Islāh' and 'Ittibah Sunnah' reformation and following the Sunnah of the Holy Prophet ﷺ. Every Hadeeth that is read should be implemented and acted upon. That is the real objective. Someone once saw Sufyān Thawri ﷺ, a great scholar of Hadeeth in a dream and he asked him, "How did Allāh ﷻ deal with you?"

He replied,

$$ ذَهَبَ الْاِشَارَاتُ وَتَاهَتِ الْعِبَارَاتُ وَلَمْ يَنْفَعْنَا اِلَّا رُكَيْعَاتٌ رَكَعْنَاهَا $$
$$ فِي جَوْفِ الَّيْلِ $$

"Indicators of knowledge have gone, texts have been destroyed, and nothing benefitted me, except the few Rak'ats of Sālatut-Tahajjud which I performed in the middle of the night."

Hence it is important to read and study Ahādeeth which contain the virtues of deeds with the intention of acting upon them and not just to know about them. That is where the real reward is. This is why Imām Ahmad Ibn Hanbal ﷺ said that there is no Hadeeth which he did not act upon. He knew over a million Ahādeeth!

Nowadays we look into the category of each ruling such as Fardh, Wājib, Sunnat, Mustahab, etc. usually acting upon the Fardh and Wājib only. But the great scholars of the past such as Imām Ahmad ﷺ would consider every instruction of the Holy Prophet ﷺ as Fardh, and acted upon it.

Knowledge is understood and cemented through actions. Implementing and acting upon what has been learnt should become second nature to the student particularly those Ahādeeth pertaining to etiquettes and manners, such as how to eat and with the correct supplications for each act. This is how the student years should become the years of reformation.

Some Useful Advice by Shaykh Ashraf Ali Thānwi ﷺ

Shaykh Ashraf Ali Thānwi ﷺ was one of the renowned scholars of his time. In one of his literatures he has offered some useful advice for the students of Deen. He said, "I address the students of Deen with utmost respect as I have some advice to offer. Your need (towards the community) is only on the account of Ilm and A'mal (practice). Without these you have no value. Remember! The more delicious a food, the quicker and more does it deteriorate and develop foul smell. Just as it is beneficial in its condition of goodness, so too will it be corrupt and harmful in its state of corruption and decay. It is therefore essential that you become concerned with your Islāh (reformation). Your Islāh can be achieved in two ways; the first is to search for a pious teacher from whom you acquire the knowledge of Deen. Never to join the company of an irreligious teacher. The time of acquiring knowledge is the period of sowing the seeds.

Secondly, after having spent some time in the acquisition of knowledge, remain in the Suhbat (company) of the Ahlullāh (the Friends of Allāh ﷻ). Only then will you acquire the correct qualification of becoming a true servant of Deen.

Nowadays, students deceive themselves with the idea that they will practice righteousness after the completion of their studies. This is totally a deception of Shaytān as it will deprive the student from doing righteous deeds. He will never gain the ability to perform good A'māl. Remember that the first impression will not return. The initial impression and effect should always be valued. The impression which one obtains while acquiring knowledge and the effect of having gained the awareness of the deeds of reward and sin are important in the initial stages. If the student takes advantage of this initial impression and acts accordingly then it will benefit him immensely. However, if he overlooks the initial

36

impression and abstains from the implementation of righteous deeds and does evil deeds then the ability will be eliminated. This ability will not return easily.

If the injunctions and severe warnings of the Holy Qur'ān and Ahādeeth, which you pursue academically, do not have an influence on your heart during your student days then what hope is there for the future. When you study during the days of the pursuit of knowledge with the intention not to implement it into A'māl, then O' my honourable friend, there is no hope that this knowledge will have a beneficial influence on you in later life."

On another occasion he stated, "Some of our students of Deen are under the false impression that 'We shall carry out good deeds after the completion of our studies.' This is totally a false notion, because the sin which you cannot abandon today, the obedience which you refuse to adopt and your deficiency in controlling (the evils) of your own Nafs which you unleash freely will only result in it increasing further in later life. Subsequently, to a greater extent you will be unable to abandon sins. Neither will you be able to adopt obedience nor control your Nafs. Therefore, you must act today (whilst engaged in the pursuit of knowledge) otherwise as time passes, Akhlāq-e-Razeelah (evil habits) will become firmly rooted (and difficult to remove). Majority of the complaints and criticisms which the general public have against the scholars are on the account of their corrupt moral behaviour. By good deeds, I am not merely referring to excessive Nawāfil, Salāh, Fasting etc, because by the grace of Allāh 🌿 you are already engaged in these acts of worship. However, the focus of my attention is not with these acts, but rather it is to do with Akhlāq.

Abandon all sins of the heart and (especially) the sins of the gaze. Be concerned in providing remedies to illnesses of the heart. Never come close to greed otherwise you will subsequently loose your value in the eyes of the people of the world. Whenever you perceive any signs of this trait (i.e. greed) then do not pursue it."

May Allāh ﷺ give us the ability to understand and enable us to act upon what the great Shaykh has mentioned, Āmeen!

Teacher's Advice to the Student

I have observed in our times many students of learning striving to attain knowledge but failing to do so, and are thus removed from its wisdom and reward. This is because they have missed the true methodology of learning by either underestimating its value or by abandoning its conditions.

Learning is indeed noble, for it leads to the fear of Allāh ﷻ which entitles the believer to receive Allāh's ﷻ eternal bliss. Learning is an adornment for the one who possesses it and a virtue to every praiseworthy action. Profit each day by increasing your learning and delving into the ocean of beneficial knowledge. Indeed, one pious person with knowledge is more powerful against Shaytān than a thousand worshippers.

Do not waste time with non-beneficial knowledge as this will cast clouds and hinder your progression towards Allāh ﷻ. Imām Abū Haneefah ﷺ said, "The purpose of learning is to act by it, whilst the purpose of action is to abandon those things that are of this life for what lasts forever."

Below is an outline of the true methods of learning which have descended from our learned and wise teachers.

1. Holding a true and noble intention and relying on Allāh ﷻ

It is necessary for the student in his/her quest for knowledge to strive for the pleasure of Allāh ﷻ, the abode of the Hereafter, the removal of ignorance from him/herself and the rest of the ignorant, the revival of religion, the benefit of Islām and not for any worldly gain. Indeed deeds are measured by their intentions. It is necessary in the quest for knowledge that one relies entirely on Allāh ﷻ and not be worried about matters like material sustenance and reduces ones attachment to worldly affairs as much as one can.

2. Respecting knowledge and those who possess it

In the pursuit of knowledge, you will not acquire knowledge nor benefit from it unless you hold knowledge in esteem and those who possess it. He who attains knowledge does not do so except through respect, while he who fails does so only by failing to respect learning and its bearers.

Sayyidunā Ali ؓ said, "I am the slave of him who teaches me one letter of the alphabet. If he so wishes, he may sell me; if he so desires, he may set me free; and if he cares to, he may employ me as a slave."

Respecting teachers requires one to avoid neither walking in front of them nor sitting in their place. The student must not speak in the presence of the teacher without permission nor to speak in any great extent without permission. In short, one should seek his approval, avoid resentment and obey his instructions in those things which are not sinful.

Remember that learning is light and purification is light, thus the light of learning is increased by purification. Respecting the books of knowledge is essential and purifying oneself with Wudhu before gaining from these books is a valued act.

Respecting learning includes respecting one's companions in the quest for knowledge and of one's fellow students. At times it may be beneficial to praise one's teachers and one's fellow students in order that one can profit from their learning.

Even if a student hears the same question and the same words a thousand times, when listening, the same respect and veneration should be given to those words. Remember, that student whose respect for knowledge after hearing it a thousand times is not equal to his respect the first time he heard it, is not worthy of that knowledge.

In seeking knowledge, it is necessary that one does not choose by himself the kind of learning and the method of learning to pursue, but to entrust the matter to the teacher and seek their approval, for surely true knowledge is a gift from Allāh ﷻ to those servants who deserve its worth and no student is worthy who mocks or complains of what he has been taught and how he has been taught.

It is an etiquette that the student does not sit too close to the teacher during a lecture except when necessary. It is better that he sits in a semi-circle at a certain distance from the teacher in a fashion that shows due respect, in an upright manner and not leaning against the wall.

41

3. Eagerness, Persistence and Exertion

These are three motivating factors in the quest for knowledge. The Holy Qur'ān states, **"Those who have earnestly striven in Our cause, We shall surely guide them to Our ways."** (29:69)

He who seeks knowledge and is eager will find it; and he who knocks at the door of knowledge and is persistent shall enter. You will reach what you desire only to the extent that you exert yourself.

One should persevere in study both at the beginning of the night and at its end, for the time between dusk and the hour of dawn is a blessed time. One should not exhaust nor weaken oneself so that one makes work difficult. One should practice moderation, for moderation is one great method for success.

Imām Abū Haneefah ﷺ said to Imām Abū Yūsuf ﷺ, "You were unlearned, but exertion in your studies made you emerge from your ignorance. But beware of laziness, for it is misfortune and a great calamity."

Finally, one should eat less as a full stomach destroys intelligence, use the Miswāk regularly as this increases memory and the ability of speaking well and more importantly it is a Sunnah of our beloved Prophet ﷺ.

4. Method of Study

It is said that learning is worth one letter, while repetition is worth a thousand letters. It is advisable that one writes down an extract of the material after memorising it and then repeats it often, for this method is indeed profitable. Imām Abū Yūsuf ﷺ had a servant, on being questioned whether she remembers anything that the learned Imām Abū Yūsuf ﷺ used to say, she replied, "Nothing except that which he used to repeat frequently."

It is important that the student makes a habit of not writing anything unless it is fully understood for this blemishes the character, reduces the intelligence and wastes time. Memorising 2 letters is better than listening to 2 loads of books; moreover, understanding 2 letters is better than memorising 2 such loads. If one becomes over-fatigued by a given subject, then he should move on to another. It is necessary not to neglect gaining understanding and praying to Allāh ﷻ and beseeching Him humbly for knowledge. Serve knowledge in a way useful to you and keep its lesson alive by good deeds.

The time for learning extends from the cradle to the grave and the best period in life for study is at the beginning of adolescence. The best period of the day to study is the time of dawn and that between the setting of the sun and the first prayer of the night.

Always remain busy in discussing with people of knowledge or fellow students about the subjects of learning in order that you may benefit. Abstain from argument, anger and hostility in forcing one's views upon another. Beware of an argument with one who nit-picks and is of undesirable character as these bad characteristics are contagious.

Sayyidunā Abdullāh Ibn Abbās ◌ was asked in what way he pursued knowledge; he answered, "With the aid of a tongue fond of asking and a heart full of good sense."

A seeker of knowledge should always be inquisitive and ask valid questions wherever he may be as the Holy Prophet ◌ said, "Wisdom is a wandering beast of the believer. Wherever he finds it, he should seize it."

One valuable way to attain knowledge is to have ink available at every occasion so that one can make notes of whatever knowledge he hears as he who simply tries to memorise what he has heard, the lesson will flee; but he who writes it down stands firm. One must carry with him a note book at all times as it is said that he who does not carry a book in his sleeve, wisdom shall not be firmly established in his heart.

Sayyidunā Ali ◌ said, "If you are occupied with learning something, then concentrate on it wholeheartedly. To withdraw from the study of knowledge of Allāh ◌ is shameful and a big loss; so seek refuge in Allāh ◌ from this distraction both night and day."

Gratitude to Allāh ◌ for the blessing of intelligence and

knowledge also increases one's knowledge. Imām Abū Haneefah
🙶 said, "I acquired knowledge by praising Allāh 🙵 and thanking
Him."

It is very important for the seeker of knowledge to seek truth from
Allāh 🙵 against error and misguidance. Those who possess wealth
should not be miserly. It is necessary to seek refuge in Allāh 🙵
from miserliness.

A person of knowledge must be sympathetic and helpful rather
than jealous, for envy is damaging and devoid of benefit.

Abstain from over-indulging in food, sleep and abundant talk
about useless matters as this will make learning easy for you and
open up the doors to beneficial knowledge. Even though your food
may be Halāl, seek food which is pure and filled with goodness;
beware of eating food in the marketplace, because this food is more
likely to be impure and contaminated.

Avoid associating with corrupt and sinful people and those who
are negligent of their religious duties or disrespectful to those of
knowledge. Choose to associate with the righteous, for closeness to
these people will leave its traces.

One should sit facing the Qiblah when studying and exert oneself
in following the etiquettes (Ādāb) of the Holy Prophet 🙲.

One should always seek the pleasure of others as the gaining of blessings of the Muslims supplications is a foundation to success.

One must engage much in Salāh and the prayers should be performed with humility as this helps the student exalt in his knowledge.

The most influential factors in strengthening one's memory are to reduce one's eating, increasing prayer at night and reading the Holy Qur'ān. Other factors are using the Miswāk, regularly drinking honey and eating raisins on an empty stomach.

Among those things that worsen memory are wrongdoing, committing sins, worrying and being anxious over worldly things and being distracted by many occupations and attachments.

Finally, always remember to pray for your teachers and parents and ask for their forgiveness as you would want them to do for you. May Allāh ﷻ make your search for knowledge a means of salvation for you and me on the Day of Judgement. Āmeen!

Shaykh Mufti Saiful Islām
Principal, Jāmiah Khātamun Nabiyyeen
August 2012, Ramadhān 1433

Other titles from JKN PUBLICATIONS

Your Questions Answered

An outstanding book written by Shaykh Mufti Saiful Islām. A very comprehensive yet simple Fatāwa book and a source of guidance that reaches out to a wider audience i.e. the English speaking Muslims. The reader will benefit from the various answers to questions based on the Laws of Islām relating to the beliefs of Islām, knowledge, Sunnah, pillars of Islām, marriage, divorce and contemporary issues.

UK RRP: £7.50

Hadeeth for Beginners

A concise Hadeeth book with various Ahādeeth that relate to basic Ibādāh and moral etiquettes in Islām accessible to a wider readership. Each Hadeeth has been presented with the Arabic text, its translation and commentary to enlighten the reader, its meaning and application in day-to-day life.

UK RRP: £3.00

Du'ā for Beginners

This book contains basic Du'ās which every Muslim should recite on a daily basis. Highly recommended to young children and adults studying at Islamic schools and Madrasahs so that one may cherish the beautiful treasure of supplications of our beloved Prophet ﷺ in one's daily life, which will ultimately bring peace and happiness in both worlds, Inshā-Allāh.

UK RRP: £2.00

How well do you know Islām?

An exciting educational book which contains 300 multiple questions and answers to help you increase your knowledge on Islām! Ideal for the whole family, especially children and adult students to learn new knowledge in an enjoyable way and cherish the treasures of knowledge that you will acquire from this book. A very beneficial tool for educational syllabus.

UK RRP: £3.00

Treasures of the Holy Qur'ān

This book entitled "Treasures of the Holy Qur'ān" has been compiled to create a stronger bond between the Holy Qur'ān and the readers. It mentions the different virtues of Sūrahs and verses from the Holy Qur'ān with the hope that the readers will increase their zeal and enthusiasm to recite and inculcate the teachings of the Holy Qur'ān into their daily lives.

UK RRP: £3.00

Other titles from JKN PUBLICATIONS

Marriage - A Complete Solution

Islām regards marriage as a great act of worship. This book has been designed to provide the fundamental teachings and guidelines of all what relates to the marital life in a simplified English language. It encapsulates in a nutshell all the marriage laws mentioned in many of the main reference books in order to facilitate their understanding and implementation.

UK RRP: £5.00

Pearls of Luqmān

This book is a comprehensive commentary of Sūrah Luqmān, written beautifully by Shaykh Mufti Saiful Islām. It offers the reader with an enquiring mind, abundance of advice, guidance, counselling and wisdom.

The reader will be enlightened by many wonderful topics and anecdotes mentioned in this book, which will create a greater understanding of the Holy Qur'ān and its wisdom. The book highlights some of the wise sayings and words of advice Luqmān ﷺ gave to his son.

UK RRP: £3.00

Arabic Grammar Beginners

This book is a study of Arabic Grammar based on the subject of Nahw (Syntax) in a simplified English format. If a student studies this book thoroughly, he/she will develop a very good foundation in this field, Inshā-Allāh. Many books have been written on this subject in various languages such as Arabic, Persian and Urdu. However, in this day and age there is a growing demand for this subject to be available in English .

UK RRP: £3.00

A Gift to My Youngsters

This treasure filled book, is a collection of Islamic stories, morals and anecdotes from the life of our beloved Prophet ﷺ, his Companions ؓ and the pious predecessors. The stories and anecdotes are based on moral and ethical values, which the reader will enjoy sharing with their peers, friends, families and loved ones.

"A Gift to My Youngsters" – is a wonderful gift presented to the readers personally, by the author himself, especially with the youngsters in mind. He has carefully selected stories and anecdotes containing beautiful morals, lessons and valuable knowledge and wisdom.

UK RRP: £5.00

Travel Companion

The beauty of this book is that it enables a person on any journey, small or distant or simply at home, to utilise their spare time to read and benefit from an exciting and vast collection of important and interesting Islamic topics and lessons. Written in simple and easy to read text, this book will immensely benefit both the newly interested person in Islām and the inquiring mind of a student expanding upon their existing knowledge. Inspiring reminders from the Holy Qur'ān and the blessed words of our beloved Prophet ﷺ beautifies each topic and will illuminate the heart of the reader. **UK RRP: £5.00**

Pearls of Wisdom

Junaid Baghdādī ﷺ once said, "Allāh ﷻ strengthens through these Islamic stories the hearts of His friends, as proven from the Qur'anic verse, **"And all that We narrate unto you of the stories of the Messengers, so as to strengthen through it your heart."** (11:120) Mālik Ibn Dinār ﷺ stated that such stories are gifts from Paradise. He also emphasised to narrate these stories as much as possible as they are gems and it is possible that an individual might find a truly rare and invaluable gem among them. **UK RRP: £6.00**

Inspirations

This book contains a compilation of selected speeches delivered by Shaykh Mufti Saiful Islām on a variety of topics such as the Holy Qur'ān, Nikāh and eating Halāl. Having previously been compiled in separate booklets, it was decided that the transcripts be gathered together in one book for the benefit of the reader. In addition to this, we have included in this book, further speeches which have not yet been printed.

UK RRP: £6.00

Gift to my Sisters

A thought provoking compilation of very interesting articles including real life stories of pious predecessors, imaginative illustrations and much more. All designed to influence and motivate mothers, sisters, wives and daughters towards an ideal Islamic lifestyle. A lifestyle referred to by our Creator, Allāh ﷻ in the Holy Qur'ān as the means to salvation and ultimate success.

UK RRP: £6.00

Gift to my Brothers

A thought provoking compilation of very interesting articles including real life stories of pious predecessors, imaginative illustrations, medical advices on intoxicants and rehabilitation and much more. All designed to influence and motivate fathers, brothers, husbands and sons towards an ideal Islamic lifestyle. A lifestyle referred to by our Creator, Allāh ﷻ in the Holy Qur'ān as the means to salvation and ultimate success.

UK RRP: £5.00

Heroes of Islām

"In the narratives there is certainly a lesson for people of intelligence (understanding)." (12:111)

A fine blend of Islamic personalities who have been recognised for leaving a lasting mark in the hearts and minds of people.

A distinguishing feature of this book is that the author has selected not only some of the most world and historically famous renowned scholars but also these lesser known and a few who have simply left behind a valuable piece of advice to their nearest and dearest. **UK RRP: £5.00**

Ask a Mufti (3 volumes)

Muslims in every generation have confronted different kinds of challenges. In-spite of that, Islām produced such luminary Ulamā who confronted and re-sponded to the challenges of their time to guide the Ummah to the straight path. "Ask A Mufti" is a comprehensive three volume fatwa book, based on the Hanafi School, covering a wide range of topics related to every aspect of human life such as belief, ritual worship, life after death and contemporary legal topics related to purity, commercial transaction, marriage, divorce, food, cosmetic, laws pertaining to women, Islamic medical ethics and much more.

UK RRP: £30.00

Should I Follow a Madhab?

Taqleed or following one of the four legal schools is not a new phenomenon. Historically, scholars of great calibre and luminaries, each one being a specialist in his own right, were known to have adhered to one of the four legal schools. It is only in the previous century that a minority group emerged advocating a se-vere ban on following one of the four major schools.

This book endeavours to address the topic of Taqleed and elucidates its im-portance and necessity in this day and age. It will also, by the Divine Will of Allāh ﷻ dispel some of the confusion surrounding this topic. **UK RRP: £5.00**

Advice for the Students of Knowledge

Allāh ﷻ describes divine knowledge in the Holy Qur'ān as a 'Light'. Amongst the qualities of light are purity and guidance. The Holy Prophet ﷺ has clearly ex-plained this concept in many blessed Ahādeeth and has also taught us many supplications in which we ask for beneficial knowledge.

This book is a golden tool for every sincere student of knowledge wishing to mould his/her character and engrain those correct qualities in order to be wor-thy of receiving the great gift of Ilm from Allāh ﷻ. **UK RRP: £3.00**

Stories for Children

"Stories for Children" - is a wonderful gift presented to the readers personally by the author himself, especially with the young children in mind. The stories are based on moral and ethical values, which the reader will enjoy sharing with their peers, friends, families and loved ones. The aim is to present to the children stories and incidents which contain moral lessons, in order to reform and correct their lives, according to the Holy Qur'ān and Sunnah.

UK RRP: £5.00